Tiny Fingers

and

Fuzzy Orange Hair

WHOSE Little Baby Are You?

Ruby Tuesday Books

by Ellen Lawrence

Published in 2016 by Ruby Tuesday Books Ltd.

Editor: Mark J. Sachner
Designer: Emma Randall
Production: John Lingham

Photo Credits:
Alamy: 7; Cosmographics: 23; FLPA: 4 (bottom), 12–13,
15–16, 17, 19; Nature Picture Library: 8–9; Shutterstock:
Cover, 1, 4 (top), 5, 6, 10, 18, 20–21, 22.

Library of Congress Control Number: 2015940232

ISBN 978-1-910549-26-1

Printed and published in the United States of America

For further information including rights and
permissions requests, please contact our Customer
Service Department at 877-337-8577.

Contents

Words shown in **bold** in the text are explained in the glossary.

A Treetop Baby

Rain forest

High in the trees of a **rain forest**, there lives a baby animal.

Mother's hand

Baby's hand

The baby has tiny fingers for holding on to her mother.

4

She has fuzzy
orange hair.

Who does this little baby belong to?

5

The little baby belongs to a mother orangutan.

The baby and her mother are resting at the top of a tree.

The tree is as tall as a six-story building.

Mother orangutan

A one-month-old orangutan

The baby orangutan cuddles
up to her mother all day
and all night.

When she's hungry,
she drinks milk from
her mother.

The mother orangutan climbs from tree to tree.

She swings on branches and **vines**.

A vine

The little baby holds
on tight as they swing
through the treetops.

When it rains, the mother orangutan makes an umbrella from leaves.

At night, she makes a cozy treetop
bed from branches and leaves.

The mother orangutan
eats fruit, flowers, leaves,
and tree bark.

When the baby is about
one year old, she tries
this grown-up food.

She eats mushed-up
fruit that her mother
has chewed for her.

The mother orangutan teaches the baby how to climb trees.

A two-year-old orangutan

As the little orangutan gets braver, she swings and climbs on her own.

Her mom is always close by, though!

The mother orangutan has lots to teach her baby.

She shows her which plants are good to eat and which are **poisonous**.

She teaches her how to build a treetop bed.

The orangutans
play and have
lots of fun, too!

19

The baby orangutan lives with her mom until she is about nine years old.

A nine-year-old orangutan

Now she is ready to take care of herself.

One day, she will be ready to have a baby of her own.

Fact File

All About Orangutans

Male orangutan

Orangutans are a type of **ape**.

An adult male orangutan has large, leathery cheek pads.

A female orangutan is ready to have a baby when she is about 15 years old.

Father orangutans do not help take care of their babies.

Orangutans eat about 300 different types of rain forest fruits.

Sometimes, orangutans eat mushrooms, bird eggs, caterpillars, spiders, and spider webs.

Orangutan Size

Woman

Female orangutan

Man

Male orangutan

Orangutan Weight

Adult male:
220 pounds (100 kg)

Adult female:
77 to 100 pounds (35–45 kg)

Newborn baby:
3 to 4 pounds (1.4–1.8 kg)

Where Do Orangutans Live?

Orangutans live wild in small areas of rain forest on the islands of Sumatra and Borneo in Southeast Asia.

Orangutans in Danger

Sometimes, people kill mother orangutans. Then they capture their babies to be sold as pets.

The rain forests where orangutans live are cut down for wood to make paper and furniture.

The forests are also cut down to make space for farmland.

Orangutans need the rain forests to be their home.

You can go online to find out how to help orangutans:
http://www.orangutans-sos.org/kids/orangutan_facts

Glossary

ape (AYP)
An animal from a group that includes orangutans, chimpanzees, bonobos, gorillas, and gibbons. Apes are very smart animals.

poisonous (POI-zuhn-uhss)
Able to harm or kill an animal or person.

rain forest (RAYN FOR-ist)
A thick forest of tall trees and other plants where lots of rain falls.

vine (VINE)
A plant with long, thin, bendy stems that grows up from the ground and gets tangled in trees.

Index

Read More

Eason, Sarah. *Orangutan (Save the...)*. New York: Rosen Publishing (2009).

Mattern, Joanne. *Orangutans (Pebble Plus)*. Mankato, MN: Capstone Press (2010).

Learn More Online

To learn more about orangutans, go to
www.rubytuesdaybooks.com/whoselittlebaby